DEPRESSION

The Path to Healing

DAN OHTEE

CONTENTS

Medication (antidepressant medications, potential side effects)

Alternative and complementary therapies (acupuncture, mindfulness-based cognitive therapy)

Chapter V. Self-Care and Coping Strategies

Healthy lifestyle habits (regular exercise, balanced diet, sleep hygiene)

Mindfulness and meditation techniques

Chapter VI. Support Systems

Family and Friends:

SUMMARY

"Depression: The Path to Healing" is an extensive manual that delves into the intricate subject of depression, providing a thorough comprehension of its origins, manifestations, diagnosis, therapeutic alternatives, and approaches for handling and conquering the illness. From a kind and impartial standpoint, the book offers a useful tool for people who want to comprehend and get over despair.

Chapter 1: Introduction

Definition of Depression:

 Persistent and severe emotions of melancholy, hopelessness, and a loss of interest in once-enjoyed activities are hallmarks of depression, a complex and multidimensional mental health illness.

It is not just a case of being "down in the dumps" or having a bad day; it is a serious medical disorder that can afflict anyone, regardless of age, gender, or background. A wide range of emotional, cognitive, and behavioral symptoms that can differ in intensity and significance are included in the diagnosis of depression.

Typical signs and symptoms include of:
- Extended depressive, empty, and hopeless sentiments
- A decline in interest in once-enjoyed activities - Modifications to sleep and eating habits
- Lethargy or low energy
- Trouble focusing or making choices
- Suicidal or fatal thoughts

Depression is a serious medical disease that has to be treated by a professional; it is not a sign of weakness or a personal failure. It is not something that can be easily "snapped out of" or defeated by determination or willpower. The definition of depression also acknowledges that various people may experience it in different ways and that there is a wide spectrum of symptoms that are specific to each person's experience.

Depression can also significantly affect a person's relationships, career, and general quality of life. It can also co-occur with other mental health issues including anxiety or substance misuse. Overall, the definition of depression emphasizes the complexity and gravity of this mental illness, as well as the significance of getting professional assistance if symptoms increase over time or continue.

Prevalence and Impact

Millions of people worldwide suffer from depression, a debilitating mental health disorder, which raises alarming concerns about its prevalence. Depression is one of the most prevalent mental health disorders in the world, affecting approximately 300 million people, according to the World Health Organization (WHO). It is projected that more than 17 million adults in the United States alone—roughly 6.7% of the adult population—have at least one major depressive episode in any given year.

Devastating effects of depression extend beyond the person experiencing it, including loved ones, the community, and society at large. Emotional pain, social isolation, subpar performance in the workplace and in school, strained relationships, and even a higher risk of suicide can result from depression. Additionally, major financial costs associated with depression might arise from missed work, increased medical costs, and decreased economic output. Anybody can experience depression, regardless of their origin, age, or gender. But some groups—women, older adults, those with a history of trauma or substance abuse, among others—are more susceptible to depression than others.

Furthermore, depression's effects might be exacerbated by co-occurring mental health issues like anxiety or substance addiction.

Depression has a variety of effects on people and society.

Emotional suffering: Severe feelings of melancholy, pessimism, and powerlessness brought on by depression can be overpowering and fatal.

- Social isolation: Depression may cause a person to retreat from relationships and social interactions, which exacerbates feelings of isolation and detachment.

- Poor performance in school and at work: Depression can impair a person's focus, judgment, and ability to finish activities, which can result in subpar work and missed chances.

- Strained relationships: Resentment and arguments can arise from depression's impact on friendships and family ties.

- Enhanced risk of suicide: Depression is a major risk factor for suicide, accounting for over 60% of suicide deaths, with mental health disorders being diagnosed in about 60% of cases.

- Financial burden: Depressive disorders can have a substantial financial impact, leading to decreased income, medical bills, and missed work.

Diminished life quality: Depression can drastically lower a person's quality of life by making daily tasks seem difficult and overwhelming.

In summary, the prevalence of depression affects millions of people globally and is a serious public health concern. Depression has a wide range of effects, impacting not just the sufferer but also their loved ones, community, and society at large.

Understanding the telltale signs and symptoms of depression is crucial, as is getting professional assistance if symptoms increase over time or continue to occur. People who receive the right care and assistance can overcome depression, which enhances life quality and lessens financial strain.

Importance of Seeking Help

Seeking help is a crucial step towards recovery from depression. Despite its importance, many individuals struggling with depression fail to seek help due to various reasons such as stigma, shame, or lack of awareness.

However, seeking help is essential for several reasons:

- Depression is a treatable condition: With the right treatment and support, individuals can and do recover from depression.

- Professional help is necessary: Depression requires professional treatment, such as therapy and medication, which can only be provided by a qualified mental health professional.

- Early intervention improves outcomes: The earlier treatment is sought, the better the chances of recovery and minimizing the impact of depression.

- Support systems are vital: Seeking help allows individuals to build a support system of loved ones, support groups, and mental health professionals, which is crucial for recovery.

- Self-care is not enough: While self-care is important, it is not enough to manage depression alone.

Professional help is necessary to develop coping strategies and work through underlying issues.

- Depression can worsen without treatment: Untreated depression can lead to worsening symptoms, increased risk of suicide, and long-term damage to relationships and daily life.

- Seeking help is a sign of strength: It takes courage to admit one needs help, and seeking help is a sign of strength, not weakness.

- Treatment can improve quality of life: Seeking help can lead to improved relationships, increased productivity, and a better overall quality of life.

- Reduced risk of suicide: Seeking help can reduce the risk of suicide, which is a leading cause of death among individuals with depression.

- Hope for recovery: Seeking help offers hope for recovery and a chance to live a fulfilling life beyond depression.

Additionally, seeking help can provide individuals with:

- A safe and non-judgmental space to share their feelings and experiences

- A professional diagnosis and treatment plan tailored to their needs

- Access to therapy, medication, and other evidence-based treatments

- Support and guidance throughout the recovery process

- A sense of control and empowerment over their mental health

- A chance to develop healthy coping mechanisms and strategies

- Improved relationships with loved ones and increased social support

- Increased self-awareness and understanding of their mental health

- A reduced risk of relapse and improved long-term outcomes.

Seeking help is a vital step towards recovery from depression. It is essential to recognize the importance of seeking help and to take action by talking to a mental health professional, building a support system, and following treatment plans. With the right help and support, individuals can overcome depression and live a happy, healthy life.

Remember, seeking help is a sign of strength, and it is never too late to ask for help. depression and live a happy, healthy life.

Additionally, seeking help can provide individuals with a sense of validation and understanding, helping to alleviate feelings of guilt, shame, and self-blame that often accompany depression. By talking to a mental health professional, individuals can gain a deeper understanding of their depression, its causes, and its effects, allowing them to develop a more compassionate and realistic perspective on themselves and their experiences.

Moreover, seeking help can provide individuals with the tools and strategies needed to manage their depression, such as cognitive-behavioral therapy (CBT), medication, or lifestyle changes. By learning effective coping mechanisms and techniques, individuals can better navigate the challenges of depression, reducing its impact on their daily lives and relationships.

Furthermore, seeking help can offer individuals a sense of hope and renewal, helping them to envision a future beyond depression. By working with a mental health professional, individuals can set realistic goals and develop a plan for achieving them, fostering a sense of purpose and direction.

In conclusion, seeking help is an essential step towards recovery from depression. It offers individuals a safe, supportive, and non-judgmental space to share their experiences, receive guidance and treatment, and develop the tools and strategies needed to manage their depression.

By seeking help, individuals can take the first step towards a brighter, more fulfilling future, free from the shackles of

depression. Remember, seeking
help is a sign of strength, and it is
never too late to ask for help.

Chapter 11: Understanding Depression

Types of depression (major depressive disorder, persistent depressive disorder, postpartum depression, seasonal affective disorder)

Depression is a complex and multifaceted mental health disorder that can manifest in different ways. While major depressive disorder (MDD) is the most well-known type of depression, there are other forms of depression that are equally important to understand. In this essay, we will explore four types of depression: major depressive disorder, persistent depressive disorder, postpartum depression, and seasonal affective disorder.

Major Depressive Disorder (MDD):

MDD is the most common type of depression, affecting millions of people worldwide. It is characterized by one or more major depressive episodes (MDEs) in a person's life, which can last for weeks, months, or even years. During an MDE, individuals experience a range of symptoms, including:

- Persistent feelings of sadness, emptiness, and hopelessness
- Loss of interest in activities that were once enjoyed
- Changes in appetite and sleep patterns
- Fatigue or loss of energy

- Difficulty concentrating or making decisions
- Thoughts of death or suicide

MDD can be further divided into subtypes, such as melancholic features, atypical features, and postpartum onset.

Persistent Depressive Disorder (PDD)

PDD, also known as dysthymia, is a type of depression that lasts for two years or more. It is characterized by a low mood and a lack of interest in activities, as well as two or more of the following symptoms:

- Changes in appetite and sleep patterns

- Fatigue or low energy
- Difficulty concentrating or
making decisions
- Feelings of worthlessness or
inadequacy
- Hopelessness

PDD is often less severe than
MDD, but it can still have a
significant impact on a person's
quality of life.

Postpartum Depression (PPD):
PPD is a type of depression that
occurs in women after childbirth.
It is estimated that up to 15% of
new mothers experience PPD,
which can manifest in the first few
months after giving birth.
Symptoms of PPD include:

- Persistent feelings of sadness, hopelessness, and helplessness
- Loss of interest in activities and relationships
- Changes in appetite and sleep patterns
- Fatigue or low energy
- Difficulty bonding with the baby
- Thoughts of harming oneself or the baby.

PPD is often linked to hormonal changes and the stress of caring for a new baby.

Seasonal Affective Disorder (SAD):
SAD is a type of depression that occurs during the winter months,

when there is less sunlight. It is estimated that up to 10% of people experience SAD, which can manifest in the following symptoms:

- Persistent feelings of sadness, hopelessness, and helplessness
- Loss of interest in activities and relationships
- Changes in appetite and sleep patterns
- Fatigue or low energy
- Weight gain
- Social withdrawal

SAD is often linked to the lack of sunlight and the disruption of the body's natural rhythms.

In conclusion, depression is a complex and multifaceted mental health disorder that can manifest in different ways. While MDD is the most well-known type of depression, PDD, PPD, and SAD are equally important to understand. By recognizing the different types of depression, we can better diagnose and treat this condition, and improve the lives of those affected.

Causes and risk factors (genetics, brain chemistry, life events, medical conditions)

Depression is a complex mental health disorder that can arise from a combination of genetic, environmental, and psychological factors. While the exact causes of depression are still not fully understood, research has identified several risk factors that can contribute to an individual's likelihood of developing the condition.

Genetics:
Genetic factors can play a significant role in the development of depression. Research has shown that individuals with a family history of depression are more likely to experience the condition themselves. This is because certain genetic mutations can affect the functioning of

neurotransmitters, such as serotonin and dopamine, which regulate mood.

Brain Chemistry:
Imbalances in brain chemistry can also contribute to depression. Neurotransmitters, such as serotonin and dopamine, play a crucial role in mood regulation. When these chemicals are out of balance, it can lead to depressive symptoms.

Life Events:
Traumatic life events, such as the loss of a loved one or a job, can trigger depression in some individuals. This is because these events can lead to feelings of sadness, hopelessness, and

helplessness, which can develop into depression if not addressed.

Medical Conditions:
Certain medical conditions, such as chronic illness, chronic pain, and sleep disorders, can also contribute to depression. This is because these conditions can lead to ongoing stress, discomfort, and disability, which can erode an individual's mental well-being.

Other risk factors:
Other risk factors for depression include:

- Age: Depression can affect anyone, regardless of age, but it is most common among individuals in their 30s and 40s.

- Gender: Women are more likely
to experience depression than
men, due to hormonal fluctuations
and social pressures.
- Social isolation: Individuals who
are socially isolated or have few
social connections are more likely
to experience depression.
- Substance abuse: Alcohol and
drug abuse can contribute to
depression, as can withdrawal
from certain substances.
- Personality traits: Individuals
with certain personality traits,
such as low self-esteem or
perfectionism, may be more prone
to depression.

Additionally, other risk factors for
depression include:

- Family history: Having a family history of depression increases an individual's risk of developing the condition.
- Social and economic factors: Poverty, unemployment, and social inequality can contribute to depression.
- Traumatic events: Experiencing traumatic events, such as physical or sexual abuse, can increase the risk of depression.
- Chronic stress: Ongoing stress, such as that experienced by caregivers or individuals in high-pressure jobs, can contribute to depression.
- Lack of social support: Individuals who lack a strong support network of friends, family,

and community may be more prone to depression.
- History of mental health conditions: Individuals with a history of anxiety disorders, post-traumatic stress disorder (PTSD), or other mental health conditions may be more likely to develop depression.
- Substance abuse: Alcohol and drug abuse can contribute to depression, as can withdrawal from certain substances.
- Personality traits: Individuals with certain personality traits, such as low self-esteem or perfectionism, may be more prone to depression.
- Environmental factors: Exposure to stressors such as noise, pollution, and poor living

conditions can contribute to
depression.

It is important to note that
depression is not a sign of
weakness, and it is not something
that individuals can simply "snap
out of." It is a serious mental
health condition that requires
professional treatment and
support.

In conclusion, depression is a
complex condition with multiple
causes and risk factors. While
some individuals may be more
prone to depression due to
genetic or environmental factors,
it is important to remember that
depression can affect anyone,
regardless of age, gender, or

background. By understanding the causes and risk factors of depression, we can better support individuals who are struggling with this condition and work towards reducing the stigma surrounding mental health.

Signs and symptoms (physical, emotional, behavioral

Depression is a complex mental health disorder that can manifest in various ways, affecting an individual's physical, emotional, and behavioral well-being. While everyone experiences depression differently, there are common signs and symptoms that can indicate its presence.

Physical Symptoms:

- Fatigue or loss of energy
- Changes in appetite or sleep
patterns
- Headaches or muscle pain
- Digestive issues, such as
constipation or nausea
- Weight gain or loss
- Changes in menstrual cycle (in
women)

Emotional Symptoms:

- Persistent feelings of sadness,
emptiness, or hopelessness
- Irritability, restlessness, or
anxiety
- Loss of interest in activities once
enjoyed

- Feelings of guilt, worthlessness, or helplessness
- Difficulty concentrating or making decisions
- Thoughts of death or suicide

Behavioral Symptoms:

- Withdrawal from social activities or relationships
- Changes in work or school performance
- Loss of interest in personal appearance or hygiene
- Engaging in self-destructive behaviors, such as substance abuse or self-harm
- Difficulty maintaining relationships or daily routines
- Increased use of technology or social media to escape emotions

It is important to note that not everyone will exhibit all of these symptoms, and some individuals may experience additional signs not listed here. If you or someone you know is experiencing several of these symptoms and they persist or worsen over time, it is essential to seek professional help from a mental health expert.

Additionally, some people may experience symptoms that are not typically associated with depression, such as:

- Physical symptoms like headaches, muscle tension, or gastrointestinal issues
- Irrational fears or phobias

- Dissociation or feeling
disconnected from oneself or the
world
- Hallucinations or delusions
- Self-harm or suicidal behaviors

It's important to remember that
everyone experiences depression
differently, and not everyone will
exhibit all of these symptoms. If
you or someone you know is
experiencing any of these
symptoms, it's important to seek
professional help from a mental
health expert.

In addition to these symptoms,
people with depression may also
experience changes in their:

- Appetite or sleep patterns

- Energy levels or motivation
- Concentration or focus
- Interest in activities or hobbies
- Social relationships or interactions
- Self-esteem or self-worth

Depression can also affect people's daily lives in various ways, such as:

- Difficulty completing tasks or meeting responsibilities
- Struggling to maintain relationships or social connections
- Experiencing conflicts with others or feeling isolated
- Having trouble coping with stress or adversity
- Feeling overwhelmed or hopeless about the future

If you or someone you know is experiencing any of these symptoms or changes, it's important to seek professional help from a mental health expert. With appropriate treatment and support, people can and do recover from depression and regain their physical, emotional, and behavioral well-being

Chapter III. Diagnosis and Assessment

Screening tools (Patient Health Questionnaire, Beck Depression Inventory)

The diagnosis and treatment of depression depend heavily on screening instruments. The Patient Health Questionnaire (PHQ) and the Beck Depression Inventory (BDI) are two frequently used screening instruments.

The Patient Health Questionnaire (PHQ): The PHQ is a self-administered tool used to evaluate the degree and existence of depression symptoms. Nine questions make up this assessment, which looks at suicidal thoughts, mood, energy, appetite, sleep, and attention. The

PHQ is a valid and dependable instrument that is frequently utilized in primary care settings.

Higher PHQ scores indicate more severe depression; the values range from 0 to 27. Major depressive disorder is indicated by a score of 10 or higher.

Beck Depression Inventory (BDI): $ The intensity of depression symptoms is gauged using the 21-item Beck Depression Inventory (BDI), a self-report tool. It evaluates suicide thoughts, mood, pessimism, guilt, and self-blame. A popular instrument in clinical and research settings is the BDI. Higher scores on the BDI indicate more severe depression;

values range from 0 to 63. Moderate to severe depression is indicated by a score of 17 or above.

 The PHQ and BDI are both helpful instruments for diagnosing depression, however they differ in a few ways:
- Length: PHQ has nine questions as opposed to 21 on the BDI.
- Scoring: PHQ scores fall between 0 and 27, whereas BDI scores fall between 0 and 63.
- Focus: The BDI evaluates symptoms over the last two weeks, whereas the PHQ concentrates on current symptoms. It's crucial to remember that these screening instruments are not diagnostic

ones, and a mental health expert should perform a thorough diagnostic assessment.

Furthermore, a wide range of contexts, including general care, mental health clinics, and research projects, have made extensive use of the PHQ and BDI. They've been demonstrated to be useful in diagnosing depression and tracking its symptoms over time. The PHQ has been very helpful in primary care settings, where it may be applied as a quick screening tool to determine which patients would benefit from more assessment and therapy. For busy primary care physicians, its simplicity and ease of administration make it a perfect tool. In contrast, the BDI has been extensively employed in research projects and mental health clinics. It is a helpful tool for mental health practitioners who need a more thorough comprehension of their patients' symptoms because of its longer format and more thorough assessment of depression symptoms. It's crucial to remember that these screening instruments are not intended to take the place of a thorough diagnostic assessment conducted by a mental health specialist. Instead, they are intended to serve as a springboard for identifying people who could be at risk for depression and need more assessment.

Apart from the PHQ and BDI, there are multiple alternative screening instruments for depression, such as the following:
- Zung Depression Self-Rating Scale (SDS)
 - Montgomery-Asberg Depression Rating Scale (MADRS)
 - Hamilton Rating Scale for Depression (HAM-D)
- Quick Inventory of Depressive Symptomatology (QIDS) The best tool to employ will rely on the particular requirements and evaluation goals.

Each of these tools has advantages and disadvantages of its own. It's also critical to keep in mind that diagnosing and treating depression is a process that begins with screening. A thorough diagnostic evaluation should be carried out to confirm the diagnosis and create a suitable treatment plan if a person tests positive for depression.

In summary, screening instruments such as the BDI and PHQ are critical tools in the diagnosis and management of depression. By employing these technologies, medical professionals can more efficiently and promptly determine which patients need additional assessment and care, leading to better mental health outcomes and more efficient patient care.

Professional evaluation (psychological evaluation, medical examination)

An essential first step in the diagnosis and treatment of depression is a professional evaluation. It entails a thorough evaluation of a person's physical and mental health conducted by a licensed physician or mental health practitioner. A physical check as well as a psychological assessment are usually part of the evaluation procedure.

Psychological Assessment: An extensive assessment of a person's mental state, encompassing their thoughts, feelings, and behaviors, is known as a psychological evaluation.

Usually carried out by a certified psychologist or psychiatrist, it could include:
- Clinical interviews: Comprehensive talks with the patient to learn about their life experiences, medical history, and symptoms.
- Psychological assessments: Standardized examinations and questionnaires to gauge the intensity of depression symptoms, such as the Hamilton Rating Scale for Depression (HAM-D) or the Beck Depression Inventory (BDI).
- Behavioral observations: Keeping an eye on the person's actions, including their affect, mood, and level of cognitive function.

Medical Assessment: A comprehensive evaluation of a person's physical health, including laboratory testing, physical symptoms, and medical history, is called a medical examination. It is usually carried out by a physician and could include:

- Medical history: An overview of the patient's past health conditions, trauma, and surgical procedures.

- Physical examination: A comprehensive physical examination that includes a review of systems, laboratory testing, and vital signs.

- Laboratory testing: To rule out underlying medical disorders that might be causing depression symptoms, use blood tests or other laboratory tests.

Why Professional Evaluation Is Done: A professional evaluation's objectives are to:
- Diagnose depression: To establish whether a person is eligible for major depressive disorder (MDD) or another type of depression.
- Discard any further conditions: to rule out any further medical or psychological issues that might be causing depression symptoms.
- Create a treatment plan: To create a suitable treatment plan that may involve counseling, medicine, or a mix of the two.

It is crucial to remember that a professional review is a continuous process rather than a one-time occurrence. Regular evaluations are required as therapy advances in order to:
- Track the intensity of symptoms
- Modify treatment regimens as necessary
- Handle any new problems or concerns.

A professional review may also entail working with additional medical specialists, including:
- Psychologists
- Social workers
- Psychiatrists
- Primary care physicians.

A thorough awareness of the patient's physical and mental health is ensured by this interdisciplinary approach, which improves therapy effectiveness and patient outcomes. To sum up, a professional assessment is an essential first step in the diagnosis and management of depression. It gives medical practitioners a comprehensive picture of a patient's physical and mental health, empowering them to create individualized treatment regimens that cater to each patient's specific needs and encourage the best possible outcome. People can get the attention and assistance they require to manage their depression and enhance their general well-being by giving priority to professional evaluation.

Differential diagnosis

The process of determining and eliminating alternative possible explanations of symptoms in order to get a conclusive diagnosis is known as differential diagnosis.

Differential diagnosis is important when it comes to depression because symptoms might mimic those of other illnesses such hypothyroidism, vitamin D insufficiency, anxiety disorders, and bipolar disorder.

The procedure of differential diagnosis includes:
1. A thorough medical background
2. A physical assessment
3. Laboratory examinations (such as blood tests and imaging investigations)
4. Psychological evaluations (such as surveys and interviews).

 Taking into account every possible reason for the symptoms, medical practitioners can:
1. Eliminate any additional disorders that might be causing or aggravating the symptoms.
2. Determine co-occurring disorders (such as anxiety and depression).

3. Create a precise treatment strategy based on the demands of the particular patient.

The following ailments could be taken into account when making a differential diagnosis of depression:
1. Anxiety disorders, such as panic disorder and generalized anxiety condition
2. Manic episodes
3. PTSD, or post-traumatic stress disorder
4. Disorder of obsessive behavior
5. Eating disorders, such as bulimia nervosa and anorexia nervosa
6. Addictions to substances
7. Medical conditions (such as chronic sickness, vitamin D

insufficiency, and hypothyroidism).

 A comprehensive differential diagnostic procedure lowers the possibility of a delayed or incorrect diagnosis and guarantees that patients receive the right care.

Differential diagnosis may also entail taking into account other mental or psychological disorders that could exhibit comparable symptoms, like:
1. Disorder of adjustment
2. Hyperactivity and attention deficit disorder (ADHD)
3. Problems with personality
4. Brain trauma

5. Neurodegenerative conditions (such as Parkinson's and Alzheimer's diseases).

It's crucial to remember that depression can co-occur with other illnesses. A careful differential diagnosis procedure can assist in determining whether any co-occurring illnesses are present.

Differential diagnosis entails a thorough assessment of the patient's symptoms, medical background, and psychiatric history. This could include:
1. Interviews with clinicians
2. Psychological evaluations (such as rating scales and questionnaires)

3. Observations of behavior
4. Laboratory examinations (such as blood tests and imaging investigations)
5. Examining psychological and physical records.

Healthcare providers can accurately diagnose patients and create a treatment plan that meets their individual needs by taking into account all possible causes of symptoms and ruling out other disorders. To sum up, differential diagnosis plays a critical role in the identification and management of depression.

A thorough assessment of the patient's symptoms, medical background, and psychological background is necessary to rule out other possible causes of the symptoms and detect any co-occurring illnesses. Healthcare providers can accurately identify patients with depression and create treatment programs that work by taking into account all possible sources of symptoms.

Chapter IV. Treatment Options

Therapy (cognitive-behavioral therapy, interpersonal therapy, psychodynamic therapy)

Treatment for depression must include therapy and there are many types of therapy that have been shown to be successful in controlling symptoms and encouraging long-term recovery. Cognitive-behavioral therapy (CBT), interpersonal therapy (IPT), and psychodynamic therapy are three popular types of therapy for depression.

CBT, or cognitive-behavioral therapy: The goal of cognitive behavioral therapy (CBT) is to recognize and alter the harmful thought patterns and actions that

lead to depression. Those that employ this problem-focused approach benefit:
- Recognize erroneous or detrimental thinking
- Crush and replace pessimistic ideas
- Create coping mechanisms and techniques
- Boost analytical capabilities CBT is a goal-oriented, structured method that usually takes 12 to 20 sessions.

Inter Personal Therapy (IPT): As relationships and communication are frequently harmed by depression, IPT places a strong emphasis on enhancing these areas. This treatment:

- Concentrates on the connections and interactions of the present
- Recognizes interpersonal problems, social isolation, or bereavement as contributing reasons
- Acquires the necessary skills to successfully express needs and emotions
- Expands networks of social support IPT, which usually consists of 12–20 sessions, is very beneficial for people who struggle with interpersonal issues.

Psychodynamic Therapy: In psychodynamic treatment, the underlying reasons and unconscious motivations of depression are examined, with particular emphasis on:

- Examining emotions and past experiences
- Recognizing coping mechanisms and defensive mechanisms
- Gaining self-awareness and understanding
- Resolving unresolved conflicts and feelings.

 This therapeutic approach may entail longer-term care and is frequently less regimented. All three of these therapies have been shown to be successful in treating depression, and the most successful strategy frequently combines aspects of each. Through consultation with a mental health expert, people can ascertain which treatment approach is most appropriate for their particular needs and situation.

Furthermore, counseling can assist people in learning coping mechanisms and techniques to control depressive symptoms, like:
- Techniques for mindfulness
- Methods for relaxation
- Techniques for managing problems;
- Communication abilities;
- Self-care routines.

Additionally, therapy can offer a secure and encouraging setting where people can process their feelings and experiences and tackle difficult problems like: Trauma, mourning, loss, and problems in relationships

Therapy can assist people in recognizing and disputing harmful thought patterns and beliefs that fuel depression, such as:
- A mindset of all or nothing
- Oversimplification Mental filter, excluding the positive, and drawing conclusions too quickly Individuals can create a customized treatment plan that fits their specific needs and goals and aids in their journey towards depression recovery by engaging with a mental health specialist.

It is imperative to acknowledge that treatment is a customized technique, meaning that an individual's preferred method may not be effective for another. To choose the best course of treatment, consulting with a mental health specialist is essential. It's critical to keep in mind that therapy is a cooperative effort between the patient and the therapist. Finding a therapist with whom you click and feel at ease sharing your ideas, emotions, and experiences is crucial.

Here are some pointers for selecting the ideal therapist: Seeking recommendations from friends, family, or your primary care physician
- Verifying with your insurance company which therapists are covered by your plan

- Investigating various forms of therapy and locating a therapist with expertise in the field you're interested in (e.g., CBT, IPT, psychodynamic therapy)
- reading internet evaluations or case studies from prior customers.

Making inquiries about a potential therapist's availability, experience, and method.

Recall that it's acceptable if it takes some time to discover the ideal therapist. It's crucial to take your time in finding a partner who can support you in reaching your objectives and with whom you feel at ease.

Apart from counseling, there are numerous other options that might assist people in handling depression, such as:
- Online forums and resources
- Support groups
- Mobile applications and internet tools
- Resources and literature for self-help
- Crisis assistance and hotlines.

Always keep in mind that getting treatment is a show of strength and that depression is nothing to be ashamed of. People can and do overcome depression and go on to enjoy happy, purposeful lives with the correct support system and treatment plan.

Medication (antidepressant medications, potential side effects)

Antidepressant medications have transformed the way depression and other mood disorders are treated, providing millions of people with hope and relief across the globe. But, they have possible negative effects and other factors to take into account, just like other medications, so it's important to fully comprehend them.

Different Antidepressant Drug Types:
1. Selective Serotonin Reuptake Inhibitors (SSRIs): These medications, which include fluoxetine (Prozac), sertraline (Zoloft), and escitalopram

(Lexapro), are among the most often prescribed antidepressants. They function by raising the brain's concentration of serotonin, a neurotransmitter involved in mood control.

2. Serotonin-Norepinephrine Reuptake Inhibitors (SNRIs): SNRIs raise serotonin and norepinephrine levels, which is another neurotransmitter linked to mood regulation. Examples of SNRIs are venlafaxine (Effexor) and duloxetine (Cymbalta).

3. Tricyclic Antidepressants (TCAs): These older antidepressants, which include nortriptyline and amitriptyline, function by preventing serotonin

and norepinephrine from being reabsorbed. Because of their increased risk of adverse effects, they are typically saved for situations in which other antidepressants have proven to be unsuccessful.

4. Monoamine Oxidase Inhibitors (MAOIs): Another class of older antidepressants, MAOIs include tranylcypromine and phenelzine. They function by blocking the enzyme monoamine oxidase, which raises serotonin, norepinephrine, and dopamine levels in the brain. They have severe food and drug interaction limitations, thus they are usually used as a last resort.

5. Atypical Antidepressants: Drugs in this group have different mechanisms of action from conventional antidepressants, such as bupropion (Wellbutrin) and mirtazapine (Remeron). For example, bupropion is typically utilized when sexual side effects from SSRIs are a concern because it predominantly impacts dopamine and norepinephrine levels.

Antidepressants may have unintended adverse effects, despite the fact that they are often very successful in treating depression.

Typical adverse effects could be:
- Dizziness and digestive problems

- Feeling sleepy or insomniac
- Dysfunction in terms of libido or inability to experience orgasm
- Increased or decreased weight
- Parched lips
- Dizziness
- Faster heartbeat
- Diarrhea or constipation.

Apart from these typical adverse effects, there may be particular dangers associated with various antidepressants. For instance, there is evidence linking SSRIs and SNRIs to a higher risk of suicide thoughts and actions, especially in young people, adolescents, and children. During the first several weeks of treatment or during dose adjustments, this risk is at its maximum.

Moreover, certain groups may experience negative consequences from certain antidepressants. For example, the possibility for orthostatic hypotension, cardiac arrhythmias, and cognitive impairment makes TCAs especially dangerous for elderly persons.

Important Points to Remember:
- Before prescribing antidepressants, medical professionals should carefully balance the dangers and advantages of each patient's unique situation.

- Patients ought to be made aware of the potential negative effects and given management advice.
- Vigilant observation is crucial, particularly in the early stages of therapy, to identify any unexpected adverse reactions or exacerbating symptoms.
- Patients must take their medications as directed and avoid stopping them suddenly as this may result in withdrawal symptoms or a depressive recurrence.

To quickly address any concerns or changes in symptoms, patients and healthcare providers must maintain open communication. Many people who suffer from depression and other mood disorders have found that antidepressant drugs have made a major difference in their quality of life. They are not a one-size-fits-all approach, though, and using them calls for thorough assessment of the unique patient circumstances as well as any possible negative consequences. Patients and healthcare providers can make well-informed decisions to maximize treatment success while reducing side effects by being aware of the many types of antidepressants, their mechanisms of action, and related dangers.

Alternative and complementary therapies (acupuncture, mindfulness-based cognitive therapy)

In order to help manage depression, complementary and alternative therapies can be utilized in addition to standard treatments.

 Among the instances are:
Acupuncture: This traditional Chinese medicine stimulates healing and balance by carefully placing tiny needles in predetermined body locations. According to research, acupuncture may be able to lessen depressive symptoms,

especially when combined with other therapies.

Mindfulness-based cognitive therapy (MBCT): This method helps people become more aware of and accepting of their thoughts and feelings by fusing cognitive-behavioral therapy with aspects of mindfulness meditation. It has been demonstrated that MBCT is useful in lowering depressive symptoms and averting relapses.

The following additional complementary and alternative therapies may be useful in the treatment of depression:
Herbal supplements (such as St. John's Wort and SAMe);
Tai Chi;

Yoga massage therapy
- Aromatherapy
- Omega-3 fatty acids.

It's crucial to remember that, even if these therapies could be beneficial, standard treatments should always be taken in addition to them after speaking with a mental health specialist.

Furthermore, it's crucial to use herbal supplements and other alternative therapies under the supervision of a licensed healthcare professional because they may have negative effects or interfere with pharmaceuticals.

Recall that the most successful depression treatment programs frequently combine conventional and complementary techniques that are customized to meet the specific needs and circumstances of each patient. A comprehensive strategy for treating depression and enhancing general well-being can be found by individuals by consulting with a mental health professional and investigating complementary and alternative therapies.

Other complementary and alternative therapies that could be beneficial for treating depression include:
Art therapy: expressing and processing emotions via artistic endeavors such as painting, sculpting, or drawing. Music

therapy: the application of music to elevate mood, ease tension, and encourage relaxation.

Animal-assisted therapy: having emotional and stress-relieving interactions with animals, like horses or dogs. Light therapy: exposing oneself to particular light wavelengths to assist in mood and circadian rhythm regulation.

 Nutritional therapy: modifying food and using supplements to promote mental well-being.

Using mindfulness practices to lower stress and enhance general wellbeing is known as mindfulness-based stress reduction, or MBSR.

It's crucial to remember that, even if these therapies could be beneficial, standard treatments should always be taken in addition to them after speaking with a mental health specialist. Locating a licensed professional with experience treating depressed patients is also crucial.

Furthermore, a few modifications to one's lifestyle can help manage depression. These include: Regular exercise: Engaging in physical activities might help lessen depressive symptoms.

Social support: getting in touch with loved ones, friends, or support networks.

Sleep hygiene: developing a calming nighttime routine and a regular sleep schedule.

Eating healthily: emphasizing complete, nourishing foods.

Recall that treating depression is a personalized, continuous process and that each person's preferred approach may differ. A thorough strategy for managing depression and enhancing general well-being can be found by individuals working with a mental health professional and investigating complementary and alternative therapies. Another few modifications to one's lifestyle can

help manage depression. These include: - Taking part in enjoyable and joyful activities;
- Developing self-compassion and self-care;
- Establishing reasonable objectives and milestones.
- Enhancing organizational and time management abilities;
 - Looking for nature and natural settings;

It's critical to keep in mind that treating depression is a journey, and doing things one step at a time is acceptable. Individuals can strive toward feeling better and enhancing their mental health by implementing tiny adjustments and utilizing complementary and alternative therapy. It's also critical to remember that depression is not something that can be "snapped out of" or conquered with effort. It's a severe mental illness that has to be supported and treated by professionals.

Seeking treatment from a licensed mental health practitioner is crucial if you or someone you love is experiencing depression. Recall that there is hope for depression's healing and recovery. Through appropriate therapy, encouragement, and self-care, people can learn to control their symptoms and enhance their general health.

Chapter V. Self-Care and Coping Strategies

Healthy lifestyle habits (regular exercise, balanced diet, sleep hygiene)

Healthy lifestyle habits are essential for maintaining overall physical and mental well-being. Three key components of a healthy lifestyle are regular exercise, a balanced diet, and good sleep hygiene.

Regular Exercise:

- Helps maintain a healthy weight
- Reduces the risk of chronic diseases, such as heart disease, diabetes, and some cancers
- Improves mental health and reduces symptoms of anxiety and depression

- Enhances sleep quality
- Increases energy levels and boosts overall physical fitness

Aim for at least 150 minutes of moderate-intensity exercise or 75 minutes of vigorous-intensity exercise per week.

Balanced Diet:

- Provides the body with essential nutrients, vitamins, and minerals
- Helps maintain a healthy weight and reduces the risk of chronic diseases
- Supports mental health and cognitive function
- Includes a variety of whole, unprocessed foods such as fruits,

vegetables, whole grains, lean proteins, and healthy fats

Aim to include a rainbow of colors on your plate to ensure a range of nutrients.

Sleep Hygiene:

- Essential for physical and mental restoration
- Helps regulate emotions and reduce stress
- Improves cognitive function and concentration
- Supports immune function and reduces inflammation
- Aim for 7-9 hours of sleep per night

Establish a relaxing bedtime routine, avoid caffeine and electronics before bedtime, and create a dark, quiet sleep environment.

Incorporating these healthy lifestyle habits into daily routine can have a significant impact on overall health and well-being. Remember, small changes can add up over time, so start with one area and build from there. Consult with a healthcare professional before making any significant changes.

Additionally, healthy lifestyle habits can also:

- Improve self-esteem and body confidence
- Enhance creativity and productivity
- Support healthy relationships and social connections
- Increase resilience and stress management
- Reduce the risk of chronic diseases, such as heart disease, stroke, and cancer
- Improve mental health and reduce symptoms of depression and anxiety
- Support healthy aging and reduce the risk of age-related diseases
- Improve cognitive function and reduce the risk of dementia

It's important to remember that developing healthy lifestyle habits takes time and effort, but the benefits are well worth it. Start by making small changes, such as:

- Taking a 10-minute walk each day
- Replacing sugary drinks with water
- Eating one more serving of fruits or vegetables each day
- Practicing deep breathing exercises before bed
- Reducing screen time by 30 minutes each day

Gradually build up to more significant changes, such as:

- Joining a gym or fitness class

- Cooking healthy meals at home
- Starting a meditation or
mindfulness practice
- Getting 7-9 hours of sleep each
night
- Quitting smoking or reducing
alcohol intake

Remember, healthy lifestyle
habits are a journey, not a
destination. Every small change
counts, and it's essential to be
patient, kind, and compassionate
with yourself along the way.

Additionally, healthy lifestyle
habits can also:

- Improve self-esteem and body
confidence

- Enhance creativity and productivity
- Support healthy relationships and social connections
- Increase resilience and stress management
- Reduce the risk of chronic diseases, such as heart disease, stroke, and cancer
- Improve mental health and reduce symptoms of depression and anxiety
- Support healthy aging and reduce the risk of age-related diseases
- Improve cognitive function and reduce the risk of dementia

It's important to remember that developing healthy lifestyle habits takes time and effort, but the benefits are well worth it. Start by making small changes, such as:

- Taking a 10-minute walk each day
- Replacing sugary drinks with water
- Eating one more serving of fruits or vegetables each day
- Practicing deep breathing exercises before bed
- Reducing screen time by 30 minutes each day

Gradually build up to more significant changes, such as:

- Joining a gym or fitness class
- Cooking healthy meals at home
- Starting a meditation or mindfulness practice

- Getting 7-9 hours of sleep each night
- Quitting smoking or reducing alcohol intake

Remember, healthy lifestyle habits are a journey, not a destination. Every small change counts, and it's essential to be patient, kind, and compassionate with yourself along the way.

By incorporating healthy lifestyle habits into your daily routine, you can improve your overall health and well-being, increase your energy levels, and enhance your quality of life. Remember to consult with a healthcare professional before making any significant changes to your lifestyle or habits.

Mindfulness and meditation techniques

Mindfulness and meditation are powerful techniques that have been practiced for centuries to cultivate mental, emotional, and physical well-being. These practices involve training the mind to focus, relax, and become more aware of the present moment.

Mindfulness:

- Involves paying attention to the present moment without judgment or distraction
- Focuses on the breath, body sensations, or emotions
- Develops awareness of thoughts, feelings, and physical sensations
- Enhances self-awareness, self-acceptance, and self-compassion

Meditation:

- Involves focusing the mind on a specific object, thought, or activity
- Aims to achieve a mentally clear and emotionally calm state
- Can involve guided imagery, visualization, or mantra repetition
- Reduces stress, anxiety, and depression

- Improves sleep, concentration, and overall well-being

Techniques:

- Body scan meditation: Focuses on physical sensations in the body
- Loving-kindness meditation: Cultivates feelings of love, compassion, and kindness
- Mindful breathing: Focuses on the breath to calm the mind
- Walking meditation: Combines physical movement with mindfulness
- Guided meditation: Follows a guided audio or visual narrative
- Transcendental meditation: Uses a mantra to quiet the mind

Benefits:

- Reduces stress, anxiety, and depression
- Improves sleep quality and duration
- Enhances emotional regulation and resilience
- Boosts mood and overall well-being
- Improves focus, concentration, and productivity
- Supports weight loss and healthy habits
- Increases self-awareness and self-acceptance

Incorporating mindfulness and meditation into your daily routine can have a profound impact on your mental, emotional, and physical health. Here are some tips to help you get started:

1. Start small: Begin with short meditation sessions of 5-10 minutes and gradually increase the duration as you become more comfortable with the practice.
2. Find a quiet space: Identify a quiet, comfortable, and distraction-free space where you can meditate without interruptions.
3. Use guided resources: Utilize guided meditation apps, videos, or audio recordings to help you get started and stay focused.
4. Focus on your breath: Bring your attention to your breath, noticing the sensation of the air entering and leaving your nostrils.

5. Be patient: Remember that meditation is a practice that takes time to develop, and it's normal for your mind to wander.

6. Make it a habit: Incorporate meditation into your daily routine, such as right after waking up or before bed.

7. Experiment with different techniques: Try various meditation techniques, such as body scan, loving-kindness, or transcendental meditation, to find what works best for you.

8. Seek community support: Join a meditation group or find a meditation buddy to help you stay motivated and accountable.

9. Be gentle with yourself: Remember that meditation is a practice, and it's okay if your

mind wanders. Gently bring your attention back to your breath or chosen meditation object.
10. Celebrate your progress: Acknowledge and celebrate your progress, no matter how small, to help motivate you to continue your meditation practice.

By incorporating mindfulness and meditation into your daily routine, you can experience profound benefits for your mental, emotional, and physical health. Remember to be patient, kind, and compassionate with yourself as you develop this powerful practice.

Additionally, mindfulness and meditation can also:

1. Improve emotional regulation: Help you better manage emotions and respond to challenging situations.
2. Enhance creativity: Increase creativity, imagination, and problem-solving skills.
3. Support addiction recovery: Aid in recovery from addiction by reducing cravings and improving emotional regulation.
4. Improve relationships: Foster empathy, communication, and understanding in personal and professional relationships.
5. Increase gray matter: Increase gray matter in areas of the brain associated with attention, emotion regulation, and memory.

6. May slow aging: Reduce cellular aging by increasing telomerase activity.

7. Increase feelings of compassion: Increase feelings of love, compassion, and kindness towards oneself and others.

8. Support weight loss: Aid in weight loss by reducing stress and increasing mindfulness around food choices.

9. Improve athletic performance: Enhance focus, concentration, and physical performance.

10. Support personal growth: Facilitate self-awareness, self-acceptance, and personal growth.

Remember, the benefits of mindfulness and meditation are numerous and can vary depending on the individual. By incorporating these practices into your daily routine, you can experience profound improvements in your mental, emotional, and physical well-being.

Chapter VI. Support Systems

Family and Friends:

A person's network of friends and family plays a critical role in managing and overcoming depression. No one is immune to the terrible mental health condition known as depression; it can strike anyone at any age or from any background. It is typified by enduring depressive and dismal feelings as well as a loss of interest in once-enjoyed activities. A robust network of support can have a big impact on how quickly someone recovers.

Advantages of a Support Network of Family and Friends for Depressed People:
- Emotional Support: Helps mitigate feelings of isolation and

loneliness by offering a sense of love, acceptance, and belonging.
- Practical Support: Assists with errands, everyday duties, and other chores to lessen workload and stress.
- Encouragement: Promotes the use of treatment regimens, self-care, and professional assistance.
- Social Connection: Promotes social engagement and lessens emotions of isolation and loneliness.
- Decreased Guilt: Assists people in realizing that depression is not their fault, which lessens emotions of shame and guilt.
- Enhanced Self-Esteem: Offers encouraging words and support, boosting confidence and self-worth.

- Coping Strategies: Provides a range of viewpoints and guidance to assist people in creating useful coping mechanisms.
- Support in Crisis: Offers a safety net in times of crisis, such as when suicide thoughts or actions occur.
- Lessened Symptoms: Research has indicated that those who have a robust support network typically have less depressive symptoms.

Creating and Sustaining a Support Network of Friends and Family for People Suffering from Depression:
- Educate Yourself: Get familiar with the signs and treatments of depression.
- Promote Open Communication: Provide a secure, accepting

environment where people can talk candidly about their emotions and challenges.

- Listen Actively: Pay close attention to what people are saying while expressing sympathy and comprehension.

- Refrain from passing judgment: Refraining from passing judgment or offering criticism might amplify emotions of shame and guilt.

- Promote Professional Assistance: Encourage people to seek out counseling and professional assistance.

- Provide Useful Assistance: Provide useful support for completing everyday duties and responsibilities.

- Have Patience: Recognize that depression recovery takes time, and have patience while the person makes improvement.

- Promote Self-Care: Assist people in engaging in self-care activities like physical activity, meditation, and hobbies.

- Seek Support for Yourself: Caring for someone with depression can be extremely taxing, so remember to receive support for yourself as well.

- Refrain from Enabling Behaviors: Recovering from an individual's behavior might be hampered by enabling behaviors like covering up or offering excuses.

- Promote a helpful Environment: Encourage relaxation and lower stress levels to create a helpful environment.

- Promote Social engagement:
Promoting social engagement and
interpersonal connections might
help fend off feelings of isolation
and loneliness.
- Provide Positive feedback:
Highlight minor successes and
accomplishments while providing
positive feedback and
encouragement.
- Respect Boundaries: Recognize
that each person's recuperation
process is distinct and treat them
with respect.
By using these suggestions,
friends and family can create a
healing atmosphere that
promotes rehabilitation and
makes depressed people feel less
isolated in their battles.

While depression rehabilitation requires time, tolerance, and understanding, people can and do recover with the correct support network.

Furthermore, friends and relatives can: Assist patients in adhering to their therapy regimens and treatment programs
- Promote good practices including consistent exercise, a balanced diet, and enough sleep.
- Offer to go with someone to therapy sessions and appointments.
- Offer people emotional support and affirmation to let them know that their emotions are recognized and valued.

- Assist people in recognizing and combating harmful mental patterns and beliefs.

-Encourage people to set and accomplish little objectives in order to boost their self-esteem and motivation.

- Promote self-care practices including yoga, meditation, and creative endeavors.

- Provide helpful assistance with everyday housework and grocery shopping.

- Refrain from passing judgment or criticism on people who are struggling and show them patience.

- Gain knowledge about depression and its management in order to comprehend what people are going through.

Urge people to get professional assistance when necessary, and offer to assist in locating options. Family and friends can be quite helpful in aiding the recovery and symptom management of persons suffering from depression by offering this kind of support. People can and do recover from depression if they have the correct support network.

Support groups (both online and physical)

Online and in-person support groups are essential for helping people deal with depression.

These communities offer a secure and encouraging setting where people may open up about their experiences, get emotional support, and interact with like-minded persons.

Personal support groups
- Provide direct communication and human connection
- Foster a feeling of belonging and community
- Permit empathy and nonverbal communication. Perhaps more successful for people who value interpersonal communication
Online forums for assistance:
- Provide comfort and accessibility from any location.
- Provide people who would like it anonymity and privacy. Permit

flexibility and access around-the-clock For people who find it difficult to leave their homes or who would rather communicate online, this might work better.

Advantages of support networks:
- Validation and emotional assistance
- Relationship with someone who can relate to what they are going through
- A feeling of inclusion and community
- Instruction and knowledge on depression and its management
- Inspiration and encouragement to seek expert assistance
- Assistance in creating self-care routines and coping mechanisms

Decreased emotions of isolation and loneliness
- Better results for mental health.

Support group types:
- Peer-led support groups: Run by people who have personally dealt with depression
- Support groups facilitated by mental health specialists
- Support groups that are issue-focused: Concentrate on certain depression-related issues, such anxiety or trauma.
- Online discussion forums and forums: Provide space for written correspondence and interaction
How to locate a group for support:
- Website of the National Alliance on Mental Illness (NAMI) The Website of Mental Health America

- The Psychology Today webpage
- Local hospitals and mental health groups
- Internet search engines.

Support groups are a complimentary tool to be used in combination with treatment, not a substitute for expert assistance. When choosing a support group, take into account the following aspects:
- Group focus: Make sure that depression and related topics are the group's main topics.
- Group style: Select a group that reflects your preferences, such as professionally guided or peer-led.
- Group size: Take into account a larger group for a range of

viewpoints or a smaller group for more individualized attention.
- Meeting frequency: Choose a group whose meetings fall on a schedule that works for you.
- Accessibility: If you prefer face-to-face engagement, consider in-person groups or, for convenience, online groups. Verify the credentials and background of the group facilitator or leader.

 Keep in mind that it could take some time to locate the ideal support group, so persistence and patience are key. If the first group you try doesn't seem like a good fit for you, don't give up; keep looking until you find one that speaks to you. For those who are depressed, support groups are a great resource. They provide a secure environment where people may connect with like-minded others, exchange stories, and get emotional support. An important first step toward healing and recovery can be taken by those who are aware of the advantages, varieties, and methods for locating a support group. Recall that support groups are meant to supplement, not to replace, professional treatment. Individuals can effectively manage their depression and achieve better mental health outcomes with the correct support group and treatment.

Furthermore, support groups can offer:

- A feeling of acceptance and kinship with people who have similar experiences with sadness
- Emotional support and affirmation, which can mitigate feelings of isolation and loneliness
- Useful guidance and recommendations from others who have overcome comparable obstacles.
-An environment free from judgment where people feel comfortable sharing their experiences and feelings.
-Possibilities for developing one's own identity and self-awareness
- Support and inspiration to adhere to self-care routines and treatment regimens

- A feeling of inspiration and hope
from witnessing others flourish
and recover.

It's crucial to keep in mind that
there isn't a single support group
that works for everyone. Instead,
people may need to try out a few
different groups before deciding
which one best suits their
requirements and preferences.
While some people might find
online groups more appealing or
convenient, others might prefer
in-person groups. Finding a group
that offers comfort, support, and
a sense of connection is ultimately
crucial.

Apart from support groups, there
exist numerous additional

resources that can assist people in managing their depression, such as:
- Mental health practitioners, such as counselors and therapists
- Internet sources and discussion boards
- Crisis and hotline numbers
- Digital tools and mobile apps
Books on self-help and educational resources

Treating depression calls for an all-encompassing strategy that incorporates social support, professional treatment, and self-care. By putting these components together, people can enhance their general mental health and well-being and lay a solid recovery foundation.

Mental health practitioners

As an essential component of their support system, mental health experts are key in helping people who are depressed. Therapists, counselors, and psychologists are among the specialists who provide clients with expert assistance, emotional support, and evidence-based therapies to help them manage depression and achieve better mental health outcomes.

Professionals in Mental Health; Types

- Therapists: Trained to assist people in recognizing and altering harmful thought patterns, actions, and coping techniques.
Counselors should concentrate on offering direction and encouragement to help people overcome obstacles in life.
Psychologists: Qualified to evaluate, identify, and manage mental health issues, such as depression.

 Functions of Specialists in Mental Health:
- Assessment and Diagnosis: Determine the cause of depression, classify its symptoms, and create a plan of care.
- Counseling and Therapy: Offer talk therapies like psychodynamic

or cognitive-behavioral therapy (CBT).

- Support and Guidance: Give people and their families emotional support, direction, and instruction.

- Treatment Planning: Create individualized plans for treatment that may involve counseling, medication, or both.

- Collaboration: To guarantee thorough care, collaborate with other medical specialists.

Working with Mental Health Professionals Has Its Advantages

- Expert Knowledge: Seek advice from qualified experts who have a wealth of experience treating depression.

- Personalized Support: Receive direction and assistance that is specifically designed to meet your requirements and concerns.
- Evidence-Based Treatments: To manage depression, access tried-and-true methods like cognitive behavioral therapy (CBT) or medication.
- Emotional Support: Find a secure, accepting environment in which to express your feelings and worries.
- Enhanced Coping Skills: Acquire practical coping mechanisms and depression management methods.
- Enhanced Self-Awareness: Acquire a better comprehension of your feelings, ideas, and actions.

Selecting the Best Mental Health
Specialist:

- Request Referrals: Speak with
friends, relatives, or medical
professionals about referrals.

- Verify licenses, qualifications,
and experience by checking
credentials.

- Research Specialties: Seek for
experts who focus on anxiety and
depression.

- Take Insurance Into Account:
Verify coverage and network
suppliers.

- Have a Consultation: Arrange a
meeting to determine comfort
level and compatibility. Experts in
mental health are vital
components of a depression
support system for sufferers. To
assist people in managing their

depression and enhancing their general mental health, they provide professional care, guidance, and emotional support.

Understanding the functions and advantages of mental health specialists will aid people take a significant step toward getting the support they require to mend and prosper.

Apart from the aforementioned advantages, mental health practitioners can additionally:
- Provide people a private, secure area to express their emotions and ideas.
- Assist them in creating constructive coping techniques

and depression management plans
- Provide assistance and direction amid trying circumstances, such a crisis or a setback.
- Assist others in establishing and pursuing their own goals
- Offer information and tools to people so they can learn more about depression and available treatments. Work together with other medical specialists to provide all-encompassing care.

It's critical to keep in mind that mental health specialists should be used in addition to social assistance from family and friends, not as a substitute for it. Joining a support group, either online or in person, can help people with depression connect with others who are going through similar things. It's crucial to: when requesting assistance from a mental health professional

- Be forthright and truthful about your emotions and experiences.
- Make inquiries and look for clarification on any issues or available treatments.
- Recognize that healing takes time and exercise patience.
- Adhere to treatment regimens and advice
- Be honest in your communication with your mental health provider about any changes or worries.

Asking for assistance from a mental health professional is a show of strength. People with depression can and can recover with the correct care and assistance.

Professionals in mental health can also assist those who suffer from depression:
- Adopt a growth mentality and become adept at reframing pessimistic ideas. - Enhance their capacity to handle stress and solve problems
- Boost their confidence and sense of self
- Establish wholesome connections and enhance communication abilities
- Control depressive symptoms, including restlessness, anxiety, and insomnia

- Acquire skills in relaxing methods like mindfulness and meditation
- Create a self-care schedule and partake in happy and fulfilling activities.
- Establish and strive toward attainable goals. Enhance their general well-being and quality of life.

It's critical to keep in mind that asking for assistance is a sign of strength, not weakness, and that depression is neither. People with depression can recover and have happy lives with the correct care and assistance. Do not hesitate to seek assistance if you or someone you know is experiencing depression.

To begin, you can: Speak with your primary care physician or other medical professional
- Making contact with a therapist or mental health expert
- Making contact with a dependable friend or relative
- Making connections with support groups and internet resources

Recall that there is hope for healing and that depression is treatable. Depression can be treated and managed so that sufferers can live happy, healthy, and productive lives.

Chapter VII. Preventing Relapse

Identifying triggers

Identifying triggers is a crucial step in managing depression. Triggers are specific events, situations, or emotions that can set off a depressive episode or worsen symptoms. By recognizing and understanding personal triggers, individuals can take proactive steps to prevent or cope with depression.

Common triggers for depression:

- Stressful life events (e.g., job loss, relationship issues, or bereavement)
- Traumatic experiences (e.g., abuse, neglect, or PTSD)
- Social isolation or loneliness

- Chronic illness or chronic pain
- Significant changes (e.g., moving, getting married, or having a child)
- Hormonal changes (e.g., puberty, menopause, or pregnancy)
- Substance abuse or withdrawal
- Certain medications or drugs
- Lack of sleep or disrupted sleep patterns
- Poor nutrition or diet
- Negative thought patterns or self-talk

How to identify triggers:

- Keep a mood journal or diary to track emotions and events
- Reflect on past experiences and patterns

- Pay attention to physical sensations and emotional responses
- Seek feedback from trusted friends, family, or mental health professionals
- Experiment with relaxation techniques and stress management strategies

Strategies for managing triggers:

- Develop coping skills and stress management techniques (e.g., mindfulness, exercise, or deep breathing)
- Build a support network and social connections
- Practice self-care and prioritize well-being

- Challenge negative thought patterns and reframe perspectives
- Set realistic goals and break tasks into manageable steps
- Seek professional help when needed

Remember, identifying and managing triggers is a personalized and ongoing process. By taking proactive steps to understand and address individual triggers, individuals can reduce the risk of depressive episodes and improve overall mental health and well-being.

Additionally, individuals can:

- Develop a self-care plan to
manage triggers
- Learn relaxation techniques,
such as progressive muscle
relaxation or visualization
- Engage in regular physical
activity to reduce stress and
anxiety
- Practice gratitude and positive
thinking
- Challenge negative thought
patterns and replace with positive
affirmations
- Seek professional help when
needed, such as therapy or
counseling
- Build resilience and learn to cope
with adversity
- Develop healthy sleep habits
and maintain a consistent sleep
schedule

- Avoid alcohol and drugs, which can worsen depression
- Stay connected with friends and family, and build a strong support network

- Practice self-compassion and challenge negative self-talk
- Engage in activities that bring joy and purpose
- Develop a growth mindset and focus on personal growth
- Learn to set healthy boundaries and prioritize self-care
- Seek professional help when needed, such as therapy or counseling
- Build a strong support network of friends, family, and loved ones
- Stay connected with others and avoid social isolation

- Practice mindfulness and presence in daily life
- Take care of physical health through regular exercise and healthy eating
- Get enough sleep and establish a consistent sleep routine
- Avoid alcohol and drugs, which can worsen depression
- Stay engaged in activities and hobbies, even when feeling unmotivated
- Practice gratitude and focus on the positive aspects of life
- Develop a sense of purpose and meaning
- Learn to forgive oneself and others
- Cultivate a sense of hope and optimism

It's important to remember that everyone's triggers are unique, and what may trigger depression in one person may not trigger it in another. By taking the time to identify and understand personal triggers, individuals can take proactive steps to manage their depression and improve their overall mental health.

In conclusion, identifying triggers is a crucial step in managing depression. By understanding what triggers depression, individuals can develop strategies to prevent or cope with depressive episodes, and improve their overall mental health and well-being. Remember, managing depression is a journey, and it's okay to take it one step at a time. With the right tools, support, and self-care, individuals can learn to manage their triggers and live a fulfilling life.

Remember, managing depression is a journey, and it's okay to take it one step at a time. With the right tools, support, and self-care, individuals can learn to manage their triggers and live a fulfilling life.

Creating a relapse prevention plan

Creating a relapse prevention plan is a crucial step in maintaining recovery from depression, anxiety, or other mental health conditions. A relapse prevention plan is a personalized strategy that helps individuals identify and manage triggers, develop coping skills, and maintain a healthy lifestyle to prevent relapse.

I. Identifying Triggers

- Keep a mood journal or diary to track emotions and events
- Reflect on past experiences and patterns
- Pay attention to physical sensations and emotional responses
- Seek feedback from trusted friends, family, or mental health professionals

II. Developing Coping Skills

- Learn relaxation techniques
(e.g., deep breathing, progressive
muscle relaxation)
- Practice mindfulness and
meditation
- Engage in regular physical
activity
- Develop problem-solving and
communication skills

III. Building a Support Network

- Surround yourself with positive
and supportive people
- Join a support group or therapy
group
- Stay connected with friends and
family

- Consider enlisting a "buddy" or accountability partner

IV. Maintaining a Healthy Lifestyle

- Establish a consistent sleep schedule
- Engage in healthy eating habits
- Avoid alcohol and drugs
- Participate in activities that bring joy and purpose

V. Managing Triggers and Cravings

- Develop a plan for coping with triggers and cravings
- Practice self-compassion and challenge negative thoughts
- Seek support from your network

- Engage in healthy coping
mechanisms (e.g., exercise,
meditation)

VI. Regular Self-Care

- Schedule regular self-care
activities (e.g., relaxation,
hobbies)
- Prioritize time for yourself
- Engage in activities that
promote relaxation and stress
reduction

VII. Ongoing Evaluation and
Adjustment

- Regularly review and update
your plan
- Evaluate what's working and
what areas need improvement

- Make adjustments as needed

By creating a comprehensive relapse prevention plan, individuals can proactively manage their mental health and reduce the risk of relapse. Remember, recovery is a journey, and maintaining a healthy lifestyle and support system is crucial for long-term success.

VIII. Seeking Professional Help

- Regular therapy sessions
- Medication management (if necessary)
- Collaboration with healthcare providers

IX. Building Resilience

- Develop coping skills and
problem-solving strategies
- Practice self-care and stress
management
- Learn to reframe negative
thoughts and emotions

X. Creating a Supportive Environment

- Surround yourself with positive
influences
- Remove triggers and negative
influences
- Create a comfortable and
relaxing living space

XI. Staying Engaged

- Participate in activities that bring joy and purpose
- Stay connected with friends and family
- Join a support group or club to expand social network

XII. Celebrating Milestones

- Acknowledge and celebrate progress
- Reflect on how far you've come
- Continue to move forward with a positive outlook

By following these steps and creating a personalized relapse prevention plan, individuals can effectively manage their mental health and maintain a fulfilling life. Remember, recovery is a journey, and it's okay to take it one step at a time. With the right tools, support, and self-care, individuals can overcome challenges and thrive.

Coping strategies and techniques

Coping strategies and techniques are essential tools for managing stress, anxiety, and other mental health challenges. These strategies help individuals develop resilience, regulate their emotions, and improve their overall well-being. In this essay, we will explore various coping strategies and techniques, including:

1. Deep Breathing Exercises: Deep breathing techniques, such as diaphragmatic breathing, can calm the mind and body.

2. Progressive Muscle Relaxation: This technique involves tensing and relaxing different muscle groups to release physical tension.

3. Mindfulness Meditation: Mindfulness practices, such as meditation and yoga, help individuals stay present and focused.

4. Grounding Techniques: Grounding techniques, like deep pressure or sensory exploration, can help individuals connect with their surroundings.

5. Journaling: Writing down thoughts and emotions can help process and release them.

6. Exercise and Physical Activity: Regular exercise can reduce stress and anxiety by releasing endorphins.

7. Social Support: Building a strong support network of friends, family, and loved ones can provide emotional support.

8. Positive Self-Talk: Practicing positive affirmations can help reframe negative thoughts and build self-esteem.

9. Self-Care: Engaging in activities that bring joy and relaxation, such as hobbies or reading, can improve mental health.

10. Problem-Solving: Developing effective problem-solving skills can help individuals tackle challenges and reduce stress.

11. Emotional Regulation: Learning to recognize and manage emotions can help individuals respond to challenging situations.

12. Self-Compassion: Practicing self-compassion and treating oneself with kindness can improve mental well-being.

13. Reframing Negative Thoughts: Challenging negative thoughts and reframing them in a positive light can improve mental health.

14. Seeking Professional Help: Knowing when to seek help from mental health professionals is essential for effective coping.

15. Mindful Movement: Engaging in physical activities like tai chi, qigong, or walking while focusing on the present moment can cultivate mindfulness and reduce stress.

16. Creative Expression: Engaging in creative activities like art, music, or writing can provide an

outlet for emotions and promote relaxation.

17. Self-Care Rituals: Developing personal self-care rituals, such as taking a relaxing bath or reading before bed, can promote relaxation and reduce stress.

18. Boundary Setting: Establishing healthy boundaries with others can help prevent emotional overload and reduce stress.

19. Emotional Awareness: Developing emotional awareness by recognizing and understanding emotions can help individuals better manage their emotions and respond to challenging situations.

20. Forgiveness Practice:
Practicing forgiveness towards
oneself and others can promote
emotional healing and reduce
stress.

21. Gratitude Practice: Focusing
on gratitude by reflecting on
positive experiences and
emotions can promote a positive
mindset and reduce stress.

22. Self-Reflection: Engaging in
regular self-reflection to identify
areas for growth and
improvement can promote
personal development and reduce
stress.

23. Building Resilience: Developing
resilience by learning from past

experiences and developing coping skills can help individuals better manage stress and adversity.

24. Seeking Social Support: Building a strong social support network and seeking help from others when needed can provide emotional support and reduce stress.

25. Practicing Self-Kindness: Treating oneself with kindness, compassion, and understanding can promote emotional well-being and reduce stress.

By incorporating these additional coping strategies and techniques into daily life, individuals can further enhance their resilience and improve their overall mental health and well-being. Remember, everyone is unique, and it's essential to experiment with different techniques to find what works best for you.

Chapter VIII. Conclusion

Summary of the Key Points

- Depression is a severe mental illness that affects children and teenagers and can have a big influence on their academic, social, and emotional growth. - It is typified by enduring depressive and hopeless feelings as well as a loss of interest in once-enjoyed activities. - The signs and symptoms of depression in children and adolescents can differ from those in adults, so it's critical to identify them in order to offer the right kind of support and care. - Depression is becoming more common among kids and teenagers, which is a rising public health concern. - Family history, traumatic experiences, long-term sickness, social isolation, peer pressure, and substance misuse are risk factors. - Making a diagnosis requires a thorough assessment that includes behavioral, psychological, and physical evaluations. - Medication, such as SSRIs and cognitive behavioral therapy (CBT), is usually used in conjunction with psychotherapy.

Hope for Recovery

- Children and teenagers can overcome depression and lead happy, healthy lives with the right care and assistance. - The likelihood of long-term negative effects can be decreased by implementing early intervention and prevention techniques, such as addressing bullying and social isolation and encouraging healthy coping mechanisms. - Access to mental health treatments and support, as well as the development of good relationships between children and their caregivers, are essential for rehabilitation. By placing a high priority on our children's mental health and wellbeing, we can assist them in building the resilience and coping mechanisms they need to face the obstacles of life. - Children and teenagers can grow and overcome depression if they are given hope and assistance.

www.ingramcontent.com/pod-product-compliance
Lightning Source LLC
Chambersburg PA
CBHW051607250726
48653CB00004BA/1384